Egypt
at the Louvre

A Guided Tour
Geneviève Pierrat-Bonnefois

In Decem...
inaugurate...
Departmen...
The two flo...   ... are
now situated ... ...e eastern wing of the
Louvre, opposite the Saint Germain
l'Auxerrois Church:

on the ground floor
Pharaonic civilisation is divided into
various sub-themes: the Nile, food and
agriculture, techniques, the home,
leisure, the temple, burial grounds,
funereal beliefs, and the gods;

on the first floor
The works are exhibited in chronolo-
gical order, emphasising three thousand
years of historical and artistic evolution.
Moreover, Egyptian works from the
Roman and Christian (Coptic) periods
are displayed on the mezzanine level of
the Denon Wing.

This itinerary seizes on various aspects
of life in Egypt, the beliefs of the
Egyptians, and ancient Egyptian
customs, via the vestiges of their
civilisation.

The tour begins at the mezzanine level.
In order to arrive there, take the
passage way under the pyramid
towards the Sully Wing. You will then
cross the moats of the Louvre fortress,
before arriving at Room 1: the crypt of
the Sphinx.

The Crypt of the Sphinx

The Great Sphinx
circa 1850 BC
Pink granite - H 1,83 m

This Sphinx represents the King of Egypt – as can be seen by the striped headdress – as a mighty lion. It was sculpted from a single block of pink granite and weighs about twenty-eight tonnes. For over a thousand years, the kings of Egypt, also called pharaohs, had their names engraved upon it. They had no scruples whatsoever about expunging their predecessors' names. Thus, the last King could easily claim that this exceptional statue, placed within and guarding the entrance to the temple, represented him. The largest of all the sphinxes, which was carved in the cliffs at the foot of the pyramids of Giza.

The great Sphinx is the guardian of the entrance to the Department of Egyptian Antiquities. It is a means of introducing us to a marvellous world, peopled with strange creatures, rigidly-postured men and refined objects. Throughout the tour, you will be sorely tempted to believe that the men who conceived and fashioned works as fantastic as the great Sphinx, for example, were just as fabulous and inaccessible as their creations. However, these men were mere mortals, like you and I, with one exception, they lived in Egypt thousands of years ago. If the objects which they left behind them seem strange, it is because their culture was so profoundly different from ours. Their means of organisation, their lifestyle, their very thoughts seemed to have been lost forever. This loss dates back fourteen centuries, to the days when the Roman emperors, who later converted to Christianity, deposed the last pharaohs. However, today, thanks to archaeologists and their work, we are now able to rediscover this civilisation, to read the texts they once wrote, and to contemplate the objects which once they fashioned.

Your guided tour goes one step further than the dream; it carries you back in time, to the vestige of a once-perished civilisation.

The Nile

Egypt is like no other country in the world, and the Nile is the longest river in the world. Its source is six thousand seven hundred kilometres to the south, in the heart of Africa, and it crosses the Sahara Desert to flow into the Mediterranean Sea. There is no one mouth of the Nile; instead its vast delta is strewn with apertures (see the map of Egypt on the back leaf). In July of each year, the Nile flooded its valley, depositing silt and fertilising the earth; today, this flooding is prevented by a dam. Rain was rare, and only the valley could be inhabited and cultivated, since it was irrigated by a network of canals which both stored and distributed water. The countryside was transformed by man into a cool, green, prosperous valley. The wilderness of the desert intruded abruptly, however, in places where no water could be conveyed. Despite its dangers, men had to venture there to exploit the quarries and mines.

A Nile vessel
circa 2000 av. BC
Stucco and paint on wood
L 67 cm · E 284

Any significant transportation was undertaken by boat, for one was never far from the river or one of its branches.
This scale model is not a toy. It was found in a sepulchre. Indeed, the Egyptians believed that the owner would thus be able to continue to go on enjoyable boating trips even after death. The owner can be seen seated in the shaded cabin, a flower in his hand, whilst the servants manoeuvre the craft.

Egyptian landscape: the desert and the fertile land

The Mastaba of Akhethotep
circa 2400 BC
Bas-relief, painted limestone

Detail of the Mastaba
Farm women carrying country produce
L (detail) 1.50 m

The mastaba is the construction which surmounted the richest tombs at the time of the great pyramids. Its interior contained a decorated chapel designed to receive visiting family members and the priests responsible for the tomb. The Egyptians believed in life after death; thus nourishment was as vital after death as it had been before.

Consequently, they used all possible means to insure their survival in the afterworld. Their meals were left in the chapel, at the foot of a magical, stone door. The souls of the dead could leave by this door, while the mummified body reposed in the underground burial vault. The chapel decorations portray work in the fields, fishing and hunting. They depict the activity of certain farms, which remained dedicated to supplying food for the dead long after the actual burial had taken place.

Egyptian life revolved around agriculture. In theory, the king owned all the land in Egypt. In practice, he rewarded his viziers by allotting them large agricultural domains, thereby making them wealthy.

The courtiers were also granted, by royal consent, the right to own tombs built and decorated by the best craftsmen of the time. The lifestyle and environment of these lords was portrayed on the walls of these tombs. Larger than the other figures, they were majestically depicted, supervising the farm workers who supplied them with food provisions.

Before entering the narrow chamber within the mastaba, do read the translations and explanations provided on the wall of the room.

Procession of offering bearers
circa 1950 BC
Stucco and paint on wood
max. height 63 cm
E 11990, E 11991, 11992, E 12001,
E 12029

These offertory bearers, in Indian file, carry out the same task as the farm women in the mastaba; they bring food to the dead. However, in this case, five hundred years later, the custom was to deposit painted wood statuettes in the tomb.

Detail of the Mastaba
Servants leading the cattle
L (detail) 80 cm

All the walls of the chapel are sculpted in shallow bas-reliefs. The representation of the subjects gives the illusion of volume, although the background is a mere three millimetres below the foreground.

The oryx, and the ibex, wild, highly strung animals, can be seen to be difficult to handle, while the oxen let themselves be led placidly on a leash.
As you will notice throughout the tour, the Egyptians were particularly skilled at representing animals.

The Meals of the Egyptians

As in days of yore or even in today's poorer countries, the Egyptian's main staples were bread and vegetables. Dates were used in the making of cakes, and fish was far more often on the menu than meat, except, of course, for the rich. "Poultry, beef, beer and wine!" – the ideal Egyptian meal during the reign of the Pharaohs – became a prayer imploring the gods to provide for the dead forevermore. The Egyptians also raised animals for pleasure; they took their dogs hunting while their cats, who were occasionally accompanied by small monkeys or even tame geese, stayed home.

Spoon in the shape
of a bound ibex
circa 1500-1295 BC
"Faience" - 11.5 cm - N 1665

Cat frolicking with
her three kittens
circa 664-332 BC
Bronze - 11.2 cm - E 5586

Both the ibex and the oryx are desert animals and the ibex was one of the hunters' favourite beasts of prey. This one can be seen captured and bound.
The Egyptians viewed the desert as a hostile, dangerous, wilderness, peopled with wild animals, similar to the forests of our fairy tales. However, both the desert and the marshes of the banks of the Nile represent Nature, and thus, an inexhaustible source of decorative motifs.

*Fragment of an inscription
painted in skilfully formed
hieroglyphics*
circa 1500-1300 BC
Painted mural on mud plaster, from the
wall of a tomb.
The details of the signs have been
restored in colour: a man walking with
a cane, a crouched, bearded god, a
human face, a seated man, his hand
over his mouth. The text, taken from a
sacred book, reads: "The great arise at
the sound of you voice, for thou art...".
L 31.5 cm - E 13099 (B)

*Seated man with papyrus paper
on his lap*
circa 2500-2350
Limestone - H 58 cm

Only those destined to work in administrative circles went to school, encouraged by their fathers who had already worked in these circles; these were the scribes. This is how the particularly lazy students were urged to study – they were constantly reminded of how difficult life was for the peasants, who had learnt neither to read nor to write, and who earned barely enough to survive and were often ill-treated.

The Egyptian writing system is more complicated than is ours. It uses approximately seven hundred hieroglyphics; some of them have different meanings.

The Ideograms
These hieroglyphics represent the object which they designate.

 represents a papyrus scroll and means "papyrus scroll". This is an ideogram and is pronounced "medjat".

 represents a star and means "star". This ideogram is pronounced "seba".

The Phonograms
For other hieroglyphics, it is the sound which lends meaning to the picture, and this sound is often much more complex than the sound of one of our letters e.g. "mut". They are used in the composition of words, with other sign-sounds, as in a rebus.

 This hieroglyph denotes the sound MN (M+N).

 This hieroglyph, an ideogram, is also used to denote the sound SBA (S+B+A).

The Determinatives
Determinative hieroglyphs, placed at the end of a word, indicate the meaning category of the word: movement, sentiment, names of men or gods, etc. They are not pronounced.

 signifies a pupil and is pronounced "sebat".

SEBA + T + the determinative which is not pronounced but which indicates the meaning category of the word – here the papyrus scroll represents writing, ideas etc. + the determinative of human being.

Now read these three examples; you will meet them during your visit:

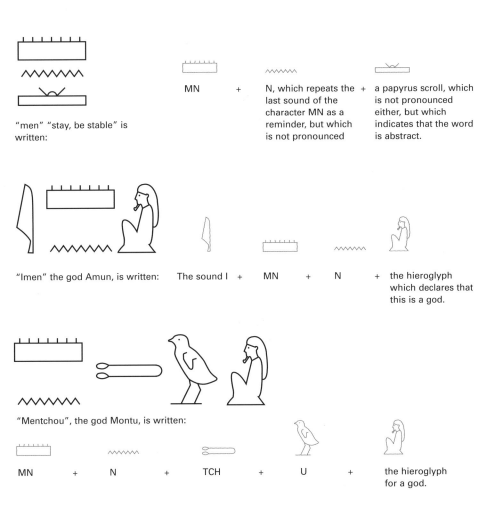

"men" "stay, be stable" is written:

MN + N, which repeats the last sound of the character MN as a reminder, but which is not pronounced + a papyrus scroll, which is not pronounced either, but which indicates that the word is abstract.

"Imen" the god Amun, is written: The sound I + MN + N + the hieroglyph which declares that this is a god.

"Mentchou", the god Montu, is written:

MN + N + TCH + U + the hieroglyph for a god.

*A carpenter's order for
windows, in cursive writing on
a fragment of pottery
circa 1200 BC
Gift from Weill - E 23554*

The scribe's writing material
*A scribe's palette with red and
black ink
circa 1330 BC
Wood - L 37 cm*

*Water pots
circa 700-500 BC
"Faience" - L 6.8 cm - N 3035*

*Papyrus cutter
Bronze - L 24.4 cm - E 3673
Gift from Tyszkiewicz*

*Schoolchild's writing tablet with a
copy of a classic in literature
"The Satire of the Trades"
circa 1200 BC
Wood - E 8424*

Writing was an administrative skill.
The harvest accounts and those of all
the property which the state managed
and redistributed, had to be recorded;
money did not exist, and wages were
paid in food and clothing.
The Egyptians also wrote letters about
their private affairs and students had to
know the literary classics. Certain
scribes specialised in domains such as
medicine and mathematics. The
hieroglyphs were jotted down quickly
using ink and paper made of papyrus,
which grew along the banks of the
river.
However, the blocks of stone engraved
with hieroglyphs which are presented
in the museum were found in temples
and cemeteries, and thus mainly
concern religion.

The Egyptians cast bronze, not only to forge tools and weapons, but also for use in the creation of sculptures and furnishings. The surface of this statue was previously hidden beneath a coat of (probably gilded) plaster, which concealed the joints of the limbs. Thus, at the time, the statue of the god Horus, arms raised to sprinkle holy water on the king, was quite extravagant. Today, however, it is austere and rather sombre, although it remains refined. In fact, the works as the Egyptians revered them, were often utterly different from what can be seen today.

The master artisan, Irtysen, both scribe and sculptor, can be seen boasting of his skills as draughtsman and artisan, on the stele hanging on the wall of this room. He was obviously proud to work for the elite, for the court and the temples. He is a prime example of the kind of men who realised the decor of the king's palace, the temples, and the religiously-meaningful tombs, as well as the more amusing designs of the furniture for the finer residences. In order to create these works of art, draughtsmen, stone cutters, sculptors, carpenters, metal casters, stuccoworkers, gilders, and ceramists often collaborated.

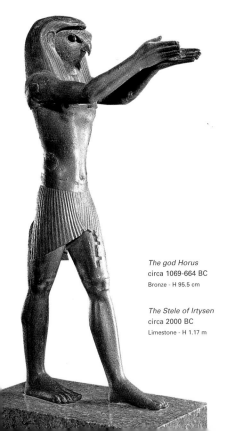

The god Horus
circa 1069-664 BC
Bronze - H 95.5 cm

The Stele of Irtysen
circa 2000 BC
Limestone - H 1.17 m

The houses were often built of mud bricks and have not withstood the test of time as well as the large, stone temples. We do know that they greatly resembled the Egyptian country homes of today, with their walled courtyards and terraces. The wealthiest abodes were enhanced by pools and gardens, which provided shade and coolness. Although it is not possible to see an Egyptian house at the museum, it is possible to discover the furnishings, which range from modest to luxurious. There are more wicker baskets than there are wooden chests, as wood was rather rare, whereas palm branches and reeds were easy to come by. Often these chests had specific functions. Some held toilette articles, frequently with compartments for cosmetics and there were chequered game chests with drawers for the draughts. The Egyptians also furnished their houses with stools, chairs, beds (although there are none at the museum), and headrests (hard pillow-like objects). They did not, however, use large tables but rather individual folding tables which were placed before each guest. Household linen, crockery and earthenware jars complete the tableau, and provide us with a picture of daily life in an Egyptian house.

Showcase of the house presenting furniture dating from the New Kingdom, circa 1550-1069 BC Wood, wickerwork, pottery

The fashionable people had all the necessary toilette articles at their disposition: mirrors, combs, hairpins, pots of cream and of kohl (used both to protect and to enhance the eyes). Traces of the cosmetics can often be found in these pots. However, traces have yet to be found on the finely-sculpted, wooden "cosmetic" spoons. Thus we remain uncertain as to their specific use. They often portray young girls by the banks of the river, pastoral scenes being especially favoured by the Egyptians. The toilette articles were often decorated with motifs drawn from nature (flowers,

desert animals, scenes from the land bordering the Nile) or with images of the protective gods. A fine example is the god Bes, who was so ugly and monstrous, he caused snakes to flee. Beauty preparations and good grooming played a major role in the lives of the rich. Hair removal and shaving were practised by women and men, respectively. They used scented oils on their skin and cosmetics, especially on their eyes. And on feast days, they donned sophisticated wigs.

Their pleated, white-linen garments required the expertise of highly-skilled laundresses. During our tour of the first-floor rooms, we shall observe the evolution of fashion over three thousand years. It was quite sober in about 2600 BC, during the time of the great pyramids, and became progressively more elaborate until Ramses (circa 1300-1100 BC).

*Spoon in the shape
of a young girl gathering
water lilies in the marshes*
circa 1400 BC
Wood - H 18 cm - N 1750

*Cosmetic tube for kohl
in the shape of the god Bes*
circa 1400 BC
"Faience" - H 8.5 cm - N 4469

Jewellery

Fish and water-lily necklace
circa 1500-1300 BC
Gold - L 49 cm - N 1852

Oudjat-eye rings
multicoloured "faience"
L 2 cm - E 17981, E 14429, AF 11053

Gold amulet of the god Thoth
H 3.45 cm - E 3876

Men and women alike, bedecked their
arms, necks, ears and fingers with
jewellery.
The goldsmiths and jewellers often
drew their inspiration from nature.
The water lily, or lotus, is omnipresent
in both the domestic and religious
decor. Jewellery was worn all day long
and its various shapes and decorations
were full of protective virtues; the
oudjat eye, signifying "to be complete,
intact" and the images of the gods are
good examples. Gold and silver
jewellery were most valuable. However,
most Egyptians wore costume jewellery,
multicoloured beads which were a
skillful imitation of the finer, more
expensive stones, such as lapis lazuli,
turquoise or carnelian.

Music played an important role in
Egyptian life. No banquet, or religious
feast could take place without calling in
the musicians. The chapel walls were
sculpted or painted with scenes depicting
orchestras playing, and dancers dancing
while the master of the house played
board games with his wife, or ate his
meal.
Although the music was not written
down, the words of several famous
songs have survived, e.g. "the harpist's
song".
The most popular game was called
senet, and its rules resembled those of
snakes and ladders.

Lyre
circa 1450 BC
Tamarisk wood - H 49.7 cm - E 14470

The lyre is a stringed
instrument, similar to a
guitar: the musician
plucked the strings which
then resonated along
wooden body of the
instrument.

Imenmes'game box
circa 1300 BC
Wood - L 36 cm - E 2710

The bottom of the box is
engraved and painted
with a draught board of
thirty squares. The
Egyptians called this
game senet; the top is
covered with a twenty-

square draught board
corresponding to another
game. On the smaller
side, Imenmes is depicted
playing senet with two
sets of counters and
knucklebones. And
within, a drawer which
no longer exists,
contained two sets of
counters for two players.

We shall now leave the world of human beings to enter the temples, which the Egyptians called "the castles of the gods".

In this immense room, the statues and fragments of walls covered in inscriptions and bas-reliefs have been arranged in such a way as to recreate the appearance of an actual Egyptian temple. Before arriving in front of the first portal, we shall follow the majestic avenue lined with sentinel-like sphinxes. Then we shall enter the first courtyard, bordered with columns adorned with colossal pharaohs. This is where the most important chancellors had permission to raise statues, and thus benefit eternally from a salutary proximity to the god. In the second courtyard, steles and inscriptions celebrate momentous political and religious events. The god, in the form of a statue, dwelt at the far end of the temple, sheltered by a small, stone chapel the *naos*. Only the serving priests had access to the *naos*, and they prayed and offered the god anything which might please him – food, incense, linen and water. The nearby secondary chapels were consecrated to other gods.

Temple relief: the King Ramses II among the gods
circa 1275 BC
Painted limestone - H 60 cm
B 11 - B 12 - B 13 - B 14

To the right, King Ramses II is led by the falcon-headed god to the other gods who hold their insignia out to him. The king can also be seen on the far left. The temples also glorified the pharaohs; if they carried out their missions satisfactorily, they would receive life, health and power in exchange. Their mission consisted in maintaining order on earth and paying tribute to the gods.

The chapel of the god
circa 550 BC
Granite H 2.55 m

The purpose of this chapel, sculpted from a single block of pink granite, was to harbour the statue of the god Osiris, at the back of the temple. It has long since lost its doors and the statue it once held. The statue represented god on earth, according to Egyptian beliefs. Every day, the priests and servants who looked after their master, opened the doors and attended to the statue; prayers and sacred music accompanied these rites.

Statue of Osiris
circa 332-30 BC
Plastered wood and bronze - H 1.68 m

Osiris is upright, wrapped
in his mummy's shroud,
hands open to hold two
sceptres, the whip and
the hook, in the manner
of the kings.

Only the Pharaoh, with the exception
of the priests, who were his representa-
tives, had access to the gods at the heart
of the temples. And only during certain
religious holidays, during the ceremony
of the procession, were the people able
to catch a glimpse of the statue. As time
went by, they became bolder and began
addressing their prayers directly to the
god of their choice.

By the beginning of the Middle
Kingdom (about 2000 BC), the god
Osiris had become very popular. It was
said that he had once reigned on earth,
transporting mankind to the heights of
happiness, but, out of jealousy, his
brother, Seth murdered him. His wife,
Isis, embalmed him, with the help of
the jackal-headed god, Anubis; thus the
first mummy was born. Osiris then
became King of the dead, while his
successor, Horus, took over on earth.
The dead pharaohs were considered to
be "Osirises". The Egyptians placed
themselves under the protection of this
benevolent, civilising god who promised
them happiness in the afterworld; they
wanted to be embalmed after death, to
become another "Osiris".

* Coffin or sarcophagus? The choice of words is a difficult one. The word coffin describes the box or case in which the body of a dead person is placed for burial, whereas sarcophagus comes from the Greek adjective meaning "which consumes the flesh". The Greeks, contrary to the Egyptians, incinerated the dead body, or en-closed it in a coffin cut from a stone which was thought to have "flesh-eating" properties, thus hastening the decomposition process. However, this is the exact opposite of what the Egyptians sought to do. Nevertheless, the word sarcophagus is often given a larger sense, designating any coffin, whether it be of stone or not, from antiquity.

A row of sarcophagi* greets you as you enter Room 14. The Egyptians liked coffins in the shape of mummies, reminding them of Osiris, the god who conquered death. This was a means of duplicating the body, which they preserved using embalming techniques. The images of the gods, and the prayer inscriptions on the coffins served to protect the body. The statues, which bore the name of the deceased, served the same purpose. The mummies, the coffins and the statues were subject to the same life-giving rituals. Thus, the statues were another form of preserving the body. These wood or stone replicas of the body were put into the tomb in the event that the mummy was destroyed. The greater the number of statue-duplicates in his or her tomb, the more chances the dead person had of resurrection... They had apertures for the mouth and eyes, thus allowing them both to eat and to see. This funer-ary ritual took place before the sarco-phagus was taken down to the tomb.

*The case of the mummy
and the coffins of Tamutnefret*
circa 1200 BC
Coated, painted and gilded wood
Max. H 1.92 m

Like Russian dolls, these coffins fit one into another. The coffins insured the best possible protection of the mummy.

19

*The Mummy of Pacheri
Wrapped in linen cloths; the
head, chest, legs and feet were
covered with heavier swathes
made of glued and painted
fabric
circa 300-330 BC
L 1.60 m*

Why did the Egyptians chose to mummify their dead? Perhaps the idea came from the desert itself. In fact, the dried out bodies buried there were already well preserved. Thus, this may be where the Egyptian's obsession with preserving dead bodies originated. The body was an important part of the whole person and had to be preserved at all costs. Unfortunately, the deep burial vaults of the more elaborate tombs could be damp, and not particularly favourable to natural preservation. Consequently, the Egyptians embalmed the body. After having carefully cleaned the corpse (removing the entrails) and dried it by artificial means (generally, by immersing it in salt), it was reshaped and wrapped in metres and metres of wound cloths.

The first illustration from "The Book of the Dead" of Khonsumes
circa 1000 BC
Painted papyri - H 26.8 cm - N 3070

Khonsumes was the chief inspector of the accountants of the temple of Amun at Karnak. He is portrayed in his beautiful pleated garment, which had been in style since the end of the New Kingdom, burning incense and offering a libation to the greatest gods of the dead: Ra and falcon-headed, Horus-of-the-Horizon, Osiris, Isis and Nephthys.

In order to insure the dead of the best possible chance of survival, amulets, protective jewellery, were left on the mummy. Depending on the time period, inside the mummy case, headrests were placed beneath the neck of the mummy, a masque upon its face, and papyrus along its legs. The papyrus was called "The Book of the Dead", and contained magical formulas to guide and protect the dead in its journey into the Underworld. In the burial vault, special furniture held small, magic statues, whose job was to do the work of the deceased for eternity. There was also a large chest containing the urns in which the embalmed entrails of the mummy were preserved. Custom once recommended placing the deceased person's lifetime furniture, chairs, baskets and vases, in the vault.

Statue of the god Bes
circa 350 BC
Limestone - H 92 cm - N 437

The appearance of the god Bes is rather special. He is a hairy gnome whose tongue is stuck out. He plays the tambourine, dances with knives in both hands, and catches snakes. His terrifying ugliness is a means of protection and he was believed to protect pregnant women, which is why he is often to be found on beds and headrests.

The numerous gods of ancient Egypt were often associated with one another in the legends. A god dwelt in the temple of a town, but that did not stop him from manifesting himself in other places. He could take on different appearances. Thus, Thoth, the god of writing and science, was a baboon, or an ibis-headed man, or an ibis, but never a baboon-headed man. Moreover, some gods borrowed the appearance of others: a falcon-headed god could be Horus or Montu. Their headdresses and, above all, the inscriptions, help to identify them.

The world of the gods was larger than that of mere human beings, and their powers were superior. The Egyptians believed that it was possible to acquire some of the gods supernatural powers by turning to magic. They used magic formulas and gestures for different purposes, including inducing a woman fall in love with them!

Mummy of a fish
Wood covered in stiff material, stucco
and paint
L 40.3 cm - N 2898 B

Mummy of a crocodile
Cloth - L 50.5 cm, 34.6 cm and 26.6 cm
N 2901, E 5832

Two cat mummies
Cloth - L 30 cm and 32.5 cm
E 2814, E 2815

These cat mummies have been examined by x-ray, allowing us to confirm that the cats were killed in order to be mummified. Specialised breeders were hard put to meet the pilgrims' demand. The pilgrims paid to have them put in these strange catacombs.

At the time of the last pharaohs, Egypt witnessed the development of a rather curious custom: the mummification of animals. In this period, the people intensified their acts of devotion in order to attract the favour of the gods. Thus small, bronze figurines of the venerated god, were left in the temple as offerings. And, in the underground galleries, situated near the great sanctuaries, thousands of mummies of the same animal piled up, offered by the pious devotees.

A Short Glossary of the Gods

Amun

Amun was the lord of Thebes, the capital of the realm during the New Kingdom. This is where the palaces and temples of Karnak and Luxor were found. His headdress consists of two long, straight feathers and a sun disk, indicating his identification with the sun-god Ra. His wife was Mut a vulture goddess, and his son is Khons, coifed with a moon disk.

Anubis

He was the patron deity of cemeteries and embalmers. All the Egyptians hoped that Anubis would come and look after their mummy as well as he had looked after the corpse and first mummy of the god Osiris. He is represented as a black dog, crouching over a tomb or at the foot of a coffin.

Bastet

This lioness goddess was as powerful and as dangerous as the wild animal itself. However, at the height of her popularity, she was considered as the goddess of the family home. Thus, she was represented with the head of a cat, playing music, and as a cat surrounded by her kittens.

Bes

This bearded gnome sticks his tongue out and brandishes his knives. However, he does this only in an attempt to frighten away any demons who might threaten the household. He cheers up the whole household by dancing and playing his tambourine. His particular function is to protect sleepers and pregnant women.

Hathor

This pre-eminent goddess was worshipped throughout the country as the patron deity of love, joy and music. She often took on the appearance of a cow, or of a woman whose face was framed by two thick plaits wound round her head and the ears of a cow. Her headdress is a sun disk held between two cow horns.

Horus

This falcon is both king of the heavens and king of men. The pharaohs were all manifestations of Horus on earth. He inherited his kingdom from his father, Osiris, after vanquishing his murderer, Seth, in a remarkable combat. He also goes by the name "child Horus" and is portrayed as a naked boy on his mother's, Isis' lap.

Isis

This great magician goddess is the wife of Osiris and the mother of child-Horus, his heir on earth. She brought him up after his father was assassinated until he was of age to avenge the murder of his father. She is represented with Horus on her lap or as a widow, lamenting the death of her husband. She protects the dead, over whom she spreads her large wings.

Maat

This goddess is the daughter of Ra, and is depicted as a woman with an ostrich feather in her hair. This hieroglyph stands for "truth" and "justice". The equilibrium of the world created by the gods reposes on these ideas. In the temples, the pharaoh is represented offering the image of Maat to the gods, signifying that he will maintain their order on earth.

Osiris

Originally, Osiris was a god of vegetation and a civilising king. After his death at the hands of Seth, Anubis and Nephthys helped his widow Isis, and invented embalming techniques for him. He became the king of the dead, and is represented shrouded. He was extremely popular as protector of the dead.

Ptah

The lord of Memphis, Ptah created the world by sheer will and word. He is the god of craftsmen and especially, of goldsmiths. He is portrayed wrapped in a coat, his head covered by a skullcap. His wife is the lioness, Sekhmet and their son, Nefertum, is portrayed with a lotus blossom. The bull, Apis, is his representative on earth, and is honoured both dead and alive.

Ra

The sun god was the source of all life. Every day he travelled through the heavens in his boat, before crossing the netherworld at night. At dawn, he is depicted as a scarab, Khepri, when the sun was at its zenith, he is associated with the falcon, Horus-of-the-horizon, and at dusk, he is Atum. Some gods united with him in order to acquire his universality.

Thoth

Portrayed with the head of an ibis or a baboon, this sage is the patron deity of writing and science. He holds his scribe's palette in his hand, and records the decisions taken in the court of Osiris, before whom appear the dead. He is associated with the moon, which can be seen on his headress, and he surveys time-measuring instruments, such as the clepsydra and the gnomon.

Three-thousand years of
Egyptian civilisation are
presented in chronologi-
cal order on the first
floor.
A timeline can be found
in the north staircase
which leads to this part
of the tour, and is of
particular help in putting
the works into their
historical perspective.

3100 BC	2700 BC				2200 BC	2033 BC		1710 B
Thinite or Early Dynastic Period	Old Kingdom				First Intermediate Period	Middle Kingdom		Second Interme Period

Dynasties	1	2	3	4	5	6	7, 8, 9, 10, 11	12	13	14, 15,
Reign	King Serpent		Djoser Sneferu Cheops Radjedef Chephren Mycerinus			Pépi II		Mentuhotep II Senusret III		

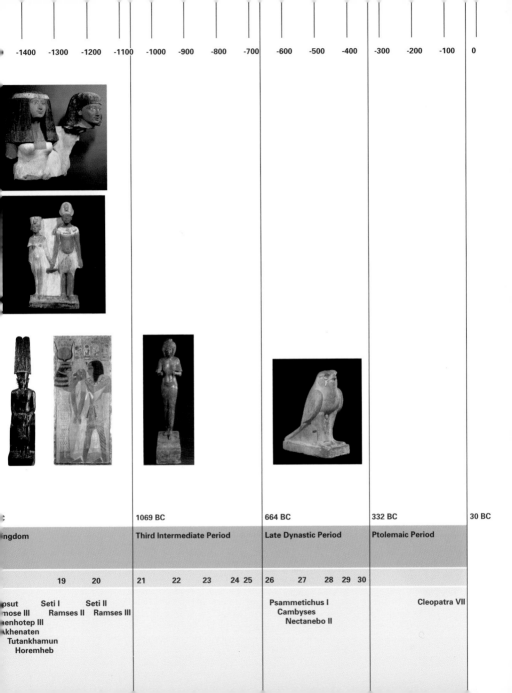

-1400 -1300 -1200 -1100 -1000 -900 -800 -700 -600 -500 -400 -300 -200 -100 0

| | 1069 BC | 664 BC | 332 BC | 30 BC |

ngdom | Third Intermediate Period | Late Dynastic Period | Ptolemaic Period |

19   20   21   22   23   24 25   26   27   28 29 30

psut   Seti I   Seti II
nose III   Ramses II   Ramses III
enhotep III
khenaten
  Tutankhamun
    Horemheb

Psammetichus I
Cambyses
Nectanebo II

Cleopatra VII

At the end of the prehistoric period, men began to cultivate the land bordering the Nile.
In about 4000 BC, they had pottery which they filled with food for the dead, demonstrating their belief in life after death. They also learnt to fashion elegant stone vases, and to work ivory, making combs, hairpins, and small statuettes of human beings. In about 3300 BC, the art of bas-relief made its apparition and could be found on ivory knife handles and stone palettes: these bas-reliefs depicted war scenes in which the chief took on the appearance of a lion or a bull. This practice was later adopted by the kings of dynastic Egypt.

The Gebel-el-Arak Knife
circa 3300 BC
Flint blade and ivory handle (hippopotamus canine tooth)
H 25.5; handle H 4.5 cm - E 11517

The artist depicted a battle scene on the side of the handle. The boats and people confront one another in superposed lines. This is a means of rendering a grandiose scene without necessarily knowing the rules of perspective. The Egyptians continued to use this process for three thousand years. There are two types of boats: round and flat bottomed. No text could possibly clearly explain who the warring parties are. Indeed, this is one of the oldest Egyptian bas-reliefs. Both the blade and the handle are exceptionally well-made.

The Egyptians first invented the art of bas-relief, and then moved on to writing. The first hieroglyphics appeared shortly before the first kings of Egypt made their apparition. They first unified Upper and Lower Egypt – "the two lands" as they were called by the Egyptians – in about 3100 BC. This period is especially known for the tombs of its kings, vast brick buildings containing hundreds of earthenware jars sealed with their names, and numerous luxury objects such as, ivory table legs and highly original stone vases.

Stele of King Serpent
circa 3000 BC
Limestone - H 1.43 m

This large stele was discovered within the tomb of King Serpent. A sculpted falcon, Horus, the god of royalty, stands at the very top. It dominates a rectangle, which represents a large wall which isturned down at the bottom; the walls of a palace can be recognised. A majestic cobra, the hieroglyph for the name of the god, can be perceived within the palace walls.

Thus it can be seen that King Serpent lived in Horus' palace; but the image is also a way of writing the name of the king in terms of Horus. Indeed, all the kings of Egypt were considered to be his successors and were called "Horus" followed by their own name. Seemingly simple, the shape and composition of the stele are, in fact, extremely subtle.

The Seated Scribe
circa 2620-2350 BC
Painted limestone
H 53.7 cm

This seated scribe, who is actually cross-legged, was an important figure of the time, whose name remains unknown. The tombs of the rich contained several statues of the same man, in different positions, alone or with his family. The poses are rigid, even when, as here, they seem to indicate action. This is because the statues represented the individual for eternity, and not his actions. At the time, the pose chosen, and the papyrus on his lap, were indicative of his high rank in society. The older statues of scribes represented the sons of kings. His eyes, inlaid with white rock crystal and white stone, and encircled with copper, bring life to the work.

In about 2700 BC, King Djoser, assisted by his architect, Imhotep, built a gigantic tomb, made, for the first time, entirely out of stone. Then, they had it raised five terraced steps. Thus, the first pyramid was born in Saqqara.
Djoser's successors, (Sneferu, Cheops, Chephren, Mycerinus) had perfect, smooth-walled pyramids built, after much trial and error. The most famous pyramids are found on the Giza plateau, near the ancient Egyptian capital of Memphis (near Cairo). The walls of the interior corridors bear no inscriptions, and we would know very little indeed about this period had it not been for the mastabas. These are the tombs of the courtiers, princes and princesses, which surround the pyramids of the kings. Within them can be found bas-reliefs and statues inscribed with texts.

Hippopotamus
circa 2000-1900 BC
"Faience" - L 20.5 cm
E 7709

This hippopotamus exemplifies the talent of those who created the works fashioned out of "faience".This consisted of powdered quartz co-vered with a glaze. During this time period the Egyptians also produced monkeys, hedgehogs, mice and statuettes of women, clothed but in belts. The beautiful blue of the hippopotamus and its seaweed design were in keeping with its environment.

Following the Old Kingdom, the country was divided among several kings: historians call this period the "First Intermediate Period". Following this, the whole country was reunited under one family.

The kings of the Middle Kingdom maintained the tradition of burials beneath the pyramids. However, their pyramids were reduced in size. Their statues provide us with impressive portraits. At this time, individuals began ordering steles of studied composition. These steles expressed the people's hope for eternal life, thanks to the intervention of the god, Osiris.

Statuette of Amenemhat III
circa 1843-1798 BC
H 21.4 cm

31

Statue of Senynefer and his wife
circa 1425-1400 BC
Painted sandstone - H 62 cm

The period in which Senynefer and his wife lived was one of stability and prosperity. This may explain the sentiment of tranquillity which one seems to be able to read in their satisfied smiles. Her face is wide and round whereas, his face is finer, and his chin more pointed. The sculptor obviously sought to render a true likeness to the originals. Their elaborate, fashionable wigs, endow them with both elegance and stateliness.

By the end of the Middle Kingdom, foreigners from the north-east, the Hyksos, had conquered half the country. The pharaohs drove them out and extended their kingdom further north and south. These countries were obliged to pay tribute to Egypt, enriching its treasury. More and more foreigners moved to Egypt and frequented its court. Luxury goods became ever more popular among the rich. Progressively, the temple of the god Amun, in the capital city of Thebes, became a veritable religious citadel, gathering its power from the booty brought back by the pharaohs subsequent to their military campaigns.

Egypt was enjoying a period of growing prosperity when King Amenhotep IV strove to free himself of the highly-influential temple of the god Amun. He attempted to impose new religious images, in which the royal family was supreme. The royal family worshipped Aten, who, in exchange, offered them life and prosperity. His sun disk was worshipped in open courtyards. Amenhotep adopted the name Akhenaten, i.e., "he who is useful to Aten", and founded a new capital, consecrated to his god, on the site of Amarna. Although this religious revolution was short lived, it did leave its mark on the artwork of the time and also "modernised" Egyptian writing.

*Amenhotep IV
and Nefertiti*
circa 1353-1337 BC
E 15593
Gift from L., I. and A. Curtis

Amenhotep IV-Akhenaten sought to revolutionise official imagery. Intimate family scenes of the king, the queen, Nefertiti, and their six daughters were depicted on steles and statuettes, which were worshipped in the houses of the capital. The portrayal of the body was particular in this time period: the king wanted the bodies of both men and women to be fuller, and their chins to jut out.

The god Amun
circa 1336-1327 BC
Diorite
H 2.20 m

The god Amun is majestic
in his tall headdress,
formed of two feathers
and a helmet. He holds a
smaller figure whose
head and hands are bro-
ken. We know, however,
that it represents a king
from the arrayal of the
remains of the striped,
royal headdress upon the
shoulders. Vandals have
not obliterated the small
cartouche (the oval fig-
ure enclosing characters
that represent the name
of a sovereign) on his
loincloth, and the name
Tutankhamun can be
clearly read. During his
reign, the god Amun
triumphed anew, and
numerous statues were
raised in his honour.
Later, worshippers
attempted to expunge all
traces of the king, under
the pretext that he
belonged to the family of
Amenhotep.

Following the reign of Amenhotep IV,
the cult of Amun, became stronger
than ever. The temple of Amun was
restored and beautiful statues of this
great god were sculpted. The facial
features given to these statues were
those of King Tutankhamun, as it was
during these troubled times that
Tutankhamun came to power. He died
at an early age and his tomb went
undetected by plunderers until it was
reopened in 1922 by archaeologist
Howard Carter and his patron,
Lord Carnarvon. It contained hundreds
of the most refined and luxurious of
objets d'art, including vases, furnishings,
jewellery, statuettes, etc.

Sudan

One of the funerary attendants of the Kushite king, Senkamanisken, found in the pyramid of the king, in Nurri, Sudan
circa 640-620 BC
Soapstone - H 20.3 cm - E 27495

The pyramids of the Kings of Meroe (Sudan)

Sudan is situated just south of Egypt. Although the successive Sudanese civilisations were different from those in Egypt, they were in close contact with one another. The pharaohs endeavoured to rule these regions in order to exploit their gold mines, but also to facilitate the acquisition of precious goods from the heart of Africa. These goods included ebony and ostrich feathers. In about 740 BC, the sovereigns of the kingdom, the Kush, conquered Egypt and reigned over the two countries for some time. They were driven back south and their successors never again ruled over Egypt. However, for generations, they continued to call themselves kings of Egypt and were buried in pyramids in conformity with Egyptian custom, accompanied by hundreds of statuettes of funerary attendants, such as the one pictured to the left.

The New Kingdom
The Reign of Ramses

King Seti I was a member of the family, of military background, which seized power shortly after the death of Tutankhamun. He was active on all fronts and strengthened the northern frontier of the kingdom in particular. One of his favourite residences was situated in the delta of the Nile. The stele in this room portrays him leaning out of the window of his palace, casting gold necklaces, in lieu of a reward, to his chancellor (the Keeper of the Seal, who controlled the royal archives). Blue-green faience tiles from his palace in the delta, are exhibited in a showcase. His son, Ramses II, at war with the Hittite Empire, made peace with this powerful rival and put a stop to hostilities for forty-six years. His long and lavish reign has endowed us with numerous monuments. Nine of his successors chose to resume this most famous of names and there were a total of eleven King Ramses in Egypt.

Seti I and the goddess Hathor
circa 1294-1279 BC
Painted limestone - B 7

The goddess Hathor welcomes the king to the land of the dead. This scene comes from the tomb of Seti I, carved into the Valley of the Kings. It was decorated entirely with extraordinarily beautiful, painted bas-reliefs, representing the afterworld.

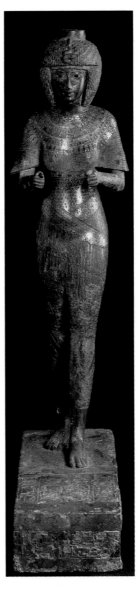

The kings of this period resided in their new capital, Tanis, situated to the north in the delta of the Nile. However, the south was governed by priests of the mighty temple of Amun at Thebes. Egypt once again found itself divided. The Libyan chieftains, followed by the Kushite kings (see p. 35) successively took over the Crown. The lords of Sais in the North, drove back the Kushite and united the country in 664. They reorganised the country and were at the origin of a new artistic impulse. However, in 525, the Persian king, Cambyse, annexed the entire Egyptian Empire after a blitz.

Karomama,
"the divine worshipper of
Amun"
circa 870-825 BC
Bronze inlaid with gold and silver
H 59.5 cm - N 500

In order to strengthen the ties between the powerful priests of Amun, who were sole masters in the region of Thebes, and the royal family, the pharaohs named one of their daughters "the divine worshipper of Amun": wife of the god and only of the god, she was invested with much temporal power in the region of Thebes. Jean-François Champollion, the hieroglyphic decipherer, brought this statue back from Egypt in 1829. He was enchanted by the silhouette and the sumptuousness of the ornamentation. It represents Koromama, "the divine worshipper of Amun", who reigned as mistress of his domain in Karnak.

Room 30   404-30 BC

From the Last
of the Egyptian Pharaohs
until the Reign of Cleopatra

The falcon Horus and the king
358-341 BC
Limestone · H 2.26 m

The falcon-god Horus protects the king, no doubt, Nectanebo II (358-341 BC) of the XXX dynasty. He was the last Egyptian pharaoh. Between the statue and the stele, slithers King Snake, king of the first dynasty, two thousand seven hundred years, and thirty dynasties

before Nectanebo. For three thousand years, the Egyptians believed that the falcon god Horus protected their king. They maintained the same language, the same writing, the same gods, and the same political system, all of which evolved progressively. Thus, may we speak of one civilisation which lasted over three thousand years.

Egypt remained under the reign of the Persians for over a century, before temporarily reacquiring independence under the last dynasties. The last Egyptian pharaohs withstood until Egypt fell once again to the Persians. Egypt was then liberated by the Macedonian king, and conqueror of the Persian Empire, Alexander the Great. He was recognised as the son of the god Amun, and therefore as King of Egypt. At his death, Ptolemy, of the same generation, succeeded him, and the country was ruled by "Greek pharaohs" for over three centuries. These "pharaohs", however, maintained the lifestyle and culture of the Greeks. The last queen of this dynasty, the celebrated Cleopatra, was defeated by the Roman, Octavius (the future Emperor Augustus)... He appropriated the country as his own personal property and the Egyptians were reduced to slavery by the Roman Empire for centuries. The foreign kings all preserved this same policy. In order to fit into Egyptian society, they acted as Egyptian pharaohs: they renovated the great temples; they had themselves portrayed on the walls of the temples garbed in the raiment of pharaohs, and in very much the same poses. They were thus able to gain the support of the priests on whom they relied to legitimise their domination. Thanks to them, the old pharaonic civilisation endured several more centuries.

Epilogue

Léon Cogniet (1794-1880)
Portrait of Champollion 1831
Canvas - H 73.5 cm; W 60 cm

The last worshippers of Isis engraved the last hieroglyphics during the 5ᵀᴴ century AD. The rest of the people had already become Christian and used the Greek alphabet. Shortly after, knowledge of writing and the religion of the pharaohs died out. Fourteen centuries later, in 1822, a scholar, Jean-François Champollion succeeded in deciphering the hieroglyphics and thus in reading the texts. He had brought the past, the long history of pharaonic civilisation, back to life. So enthusiastic was he that he managed to convince King Charles X to open an Egyptian Antiquities gallery at the Louvre. Thus it is that 19ᵀᴴ century Europeans were able to discover this rich culture of antiquity, which preceded those of the Greeks and the Romans. And he thus, provided us with the possibility of approaching this testimony to the past, which opens the doors to a long-gone world.

Léon Cogniet (1794-1880)
Ceiling decoration of room 44, detail
Bonaparte, surrounded by scholars and artists, present at the discover of a mummy 1835

Louvre Museum, Paris, 1997
Chercheurs d'art Collection

Conceived, coordinated and created by:
Violaine Bouvet-Lanselle,
Department of Culture

**Egypt at the Louvre
A guided tour**
by Geneviève Pierrat-Bonnefois
Curator in the Department of Egyptian Antiquities at the Louvre Museum

Graphics conceived by:
Agathe Hondré,
Louvre Museum
Vincent Grousson
Supervision, Philippe Apeloig

Publishing secretary:
Cécile Dufêtre,
Louvre Museum
Marie-Dominique de Teneuille

Translation:
Translated from the French by Jennifer McWha

Illustrations:
Catherine Bridonneau,
Department of Egyptian Antiquities
Isabelle Gaëtan,
Department of Culture

Drawings for the Glossary of the gods:
Catherine Adam,
Laurence Michel

Louvre graphics workshop coordinator:
Anne-Louise Cavillon

RMN production supervisor:
Jacques Venelli

Photography credits:
Jean-Michel Charbonnier,
p. 35 ; Maurice et Pierre Chuzeville / musée du Louvre,
p. 5, 22, 31 ;. Christian Larrieu / musée du Louvre,
p. 7, 12, 14, 16-17, 33, 38 ;
Christian Larrieu / La Licorne,
p. 4 ; Geneviève Pierrat, p. 3 ;
Étienne Revault / musée du Louvre, p. 39 ; RMN : 6, 11, 30, 34, 37 ; RMN / Arnaudet : p. 29 ;
RMN / Chuzeville : p. 2, 10, 15, 17, 19-21, 32, 36 ; RMN / Lewandowski : p. 3, 5-6, 11, 13-14, 18, 23, 28, 31, 35 ; RMN / Blot : p. 39 ; RMN / Lebée : p. 13 RMN / Ojeda : p. 10

Photoengraving:
I. G. S. - CP Angoulême

© Éditions de la Réunion des musées nationaux, Paris, 1998
49, rue Etienne Marcel
75001 Paris

Printed in July 1998
by Mussot

Dépôt légal : July 1998
ISSN 1142-334 X
ISBN 2-7118-3746-7

LOUVRE

Réunion
des Musées
Nationaux